Bold and Virtuous Project Leadership

Randall Calloway

Though I speak with the tongues of men and of angels and have not love………I am nothing. I Cor.13:1-2

This effort is dedicated to my wife, Jonizo, and my parents, Marshall and Elizabeth. Thanks for everything.

Bold and Virtuous Project Leadership

Chapter 1

The Backdrop

It is April, 1940, and most of the civilized world is at war. In the Far East, the armies of Imperial Japan have invaded several countries, including the nation of China. During 1939, the "Rape" of Nan King was one of their most violent atrocities, but not the only one. Japan was stretching its power and influence in a strident attempt to gain natural resources and enhance its standing as a world class power, still attempting to overcome embarrassments in the previous century when it was a predominantly agricultural nation , albeit one with rich intellectual and artistic history. In the intervening years since Admiral Perry's proud entrance into Tokyo Bay with the American Far Eastern Fleet, it had not only become a world class industrial nation, it had built the world's most formidable and modern navy, complete with the highest technology warship of the day, the aircraft carrier. The threat from Japan to peaceful countries is so felt in free nations that American pilots are volunteering for duty with Chiang- Kai-shek, the leader of the Republic of China, to comprise the "Flying Tigers", an air squadron attempting to hamper the

Japanese war effort in China and to support the free Chinese in their fight against the aggressor nation.

In Europe, the Spanish Civil War of 1937 had been a time for Hitler to test his war machine and fine tune it for further exploits. Soon, in 1939, he took the Sudetenland, a disputed portion of Czechoslovakia, then began his lightning war, *Blitzkrieg,* to overrun Poland. This attack triggered the treaty bound response from England and France, and war was declared soon after the invasion. It did not take long for England to send troops to help defend France. It took even less time for the armies of Third Reich to bypass the Maginot line and use air power and lightning fast mechanized ground forces to pick the French defenses apart. By June of 1940, the entire British Army will be retreating across the English Channel in the most stunning naval rescue operation ever conceived, the rescue of British and Free French forces with the "little boats" at Dunkirk. They would use hundreds of civilian craft and every available boat to cross the channel and remove the beleaguered soldiers from the beaches at Dunkirk.

The war tensions are forcing Americans to pick a side, although, before the Pearl Harbor attack in December of '41, most Americans are against involvement in another war, remembering the hundreds of thousands of American casualties in the "Great War", World War I.

Although the official position is neutrality, Americans are generally aware that war is looming for them as well. President Roosevelt is committed to making America the "Arsenal of Democracy", and gearing up design and production of war materiel to support the English in their fight against Hitler. In that regard, it is becoming apparent that the next great war will be fought with new technology and that if the lightning overruns of Poland and France are any indicator, a large portion of that technology will include air power. Since the last war, aircraft technology has progressed steadily. Biplanes that would fly at 100 mph have been surpassed by closed cockpit monoplanes with retractable landing gear that fly at over 300 mph. Multiple engine troop transports and bombers are being used by the Germans and Japanese. High altitude bombing capabilities are causing defense planners to seek new high altitude fighters that could be used in defense against these new powerful bombers. Although they do not know it, it will only be a matter of months before the Battle of Britain begins with the night bombing of English defense factories and cities.

In the United States several new aircraft are being designed to meet this presumed challenge. One of the best single engine American production fighter aircraft available in April, 1940, is the Curtiss Aircraft P-40 Warhawk, or Tomahawk, being used by Chiang- Kai-shek and the "Flying Tigers", under the command of Claire Chennault. Although this is one of the best America has, it is slower than the Japanese Zero, and generally less maneuverable, although much more rugged. Skilled pilots can use its advantages against the enemy such as the ability to dive faster and its heavier armament. It was designed in 1937, so even it is becoming dated and near obsolete.

It is against this backdrop that one of the most fascinating stories of dynamic and bold business leadership is set.

The British Defense Ministry is coming to the US to buy fighters. They, of course, want the most fighter for their money, so they are placing orders for the Curtiss P-40. They are asking other aircraft manufacturers to subcontract production of the fighter, as Curtis Aircraft is overloaded and cannot meet the aggressive British schedule. (Pearcy, 1996, p.30)

Evacuating British and Free French troops in the "little boats", at Dunkirk, 1940

Chapter 2

The Story

What would become one of the most eventful days in aviation history was the day the British Defense Ministry personnel met the president of North American Aviation, James Howard Kindelberger. "Dutch" Kindelberger had risen to be chief of North American Aviation, if you will, organically. Unlike some corporate chieftains, he was not a generic CEO, subject to move between corporations in different industries, supplying key executive management skills necessary in any type of business. No, Dutch was an airplane guy. He did, however, have some key skills that will be discussed later that were indeed transferrable to any enterprise, even to the extent that they could be described as life success secrets. He was a person who loved all things about aviation. He was born in 1895 in Wheeling, West Virginia, to German immigrants from Nothweiler, Pfalz. From them he had learned values that would serve him well in corporate management. He served in the US Army Air Service in World War I. It is there he picked up a love of flying and aircraft.

After World War I, he studied engineering and went to work in the aircraft industry, finally arriving at Douglas Aircraft in 1930. There he met Lee Atwood, forming what would be a lifelong collaborative professional friendship. There they worked on the DC-1 and DC-2 Transports. They left Douglas Aircraft in 1934, coming to North American Aviation in the manufacturing division. The company had only one aircraft on order when they arrived. Somehow, Dutch managed to get an order booked for the BT-9 aircraft. He was a people person, and soon rose to be President of North American. His friend and associate Lee Atwood became Chief Engineer. Together, along with a uniquely talented team, they would make aviation history, and we can learn some key success lessons from this effort.

The British sensed a looming attack on Britain, that most certainly would include an air assault. German bombers would be headed for the skies over England, and they needed fighters, the best that could be had. The best the Americans had to offer at the time was the P-40 Warhawk, by Curtiss Aircraft. The British asked North American to produce an order of the fighters, licensing production from Curtiss. This would be a certain profit with no risk, and any modern-era CEO should have grabbed the low risk profit opportunity and asked for more. Dutch Kindelberger wanted none of it. Instead, he saw this as a grand opportunity to design his own aircraft for the same service and produce the best fighter yet designed. The Warhawk was a 1937 design, and he knew he could best it, particularly with a certain set of "aces" he knew he had up his sleeve. (Are we sure he wasn't from Texas? Maybe he was a fan of Western movies.)

It is hard to believe he didn't have a flair for the dramatic, as we look back at this notion from the perspective of hindsight. Just imagine the response of the British procurement officers as they hear his proposal. They have just offered a guaranteed profit to a CEO of a company in a country that is still in a depression. He doesn't want the deal, but makes a risky counter offer to design a plane from scratch, that he brashly postulates will outperform the best American single engine fighter in existence. They recall that they are charged with a mission to defend England from an imminent threat, and they don't have any time to wait for a normal development effort. But here is an American CEO with significant experience in the business of aviation, assuring them he can develop a faster fighter in a short period of time. They really would like to have the fastest fighter they could get their hands on. But what about the risk to Britain's defenses if the delay is not productive, if the fighter is no faster, or falls apart in the first trials? To this question they apparently decided that the production of a conventional run of Warhawks would be soon enough to meet requirements, even with the delay, given it was a settled design. Perhaps they determined they could get the conventional fighters from other sub contractors if this gamble didn't pan out. They agree to a 120 day delivery of a flying, fully functional prototype, which had to be faster than the Warhawk or no deal. They figure they can't lose, they either get a faster plane, or they get the conventional fighter. The race against time is on.

Just what is Dutch Kindelbeger thinking? Certainly he knows it normally takes a year on a fast track program to develop a world class fighter. What makes him think that he should be risking the profits of his company this way? After all, this is a public corporation, not his private company. He answers to a board of directors. Is this decision bordering on ludicrous? What are the "aces" he has up his sleeve? We can only imagine what the board of directors would say at the next quarterly review if he told them the full extent of the deal. What kind of CEO would risk his career in such an endeavor? Not many CEO's of today would do this. Not many in that day would have done it either. But we must remember, Dutch is an airplane guy first, a calculating risk taker second, and a CEO third. Wow, this is unconventional! Who of us has ever worked for this type of company? Who secretly wishes they did? Is this serious drama or what? The defense of a nation hangs in the balance, the risks of development are high, and yet he offers this gambit. Just think of the options he could have chosen. He could have taken the subcontract fabrication, and allocated a small portion of the profits for development of the new experimental fighter. Wouldn't this be the prudent course of action that the board of directors would have viewed as aggressive yet pragmatic? He could have even taken the conventional contract and developed the new fighter on paper, and in the wind tunnel, at very low cost and risk? What would have been the outcome of these alternate choices?

Typically, these less radical initiatives would have taken longer to come to fruition, and perhaps the fighter would have never even flown. The support for the development of a fully functional prototype may not have been offered. A conservative governance of the corporation usually opts for sure profits rather than risky ventures. The company may have made great profits simply subcontracting fabrication of the designs of others. It may have even created a successful niche business doing just that, offering proven "excellence" in manufacturing rather than risky new design development. There is really nothing wrong at all with that type of corporate mission. Great wealth is often created in fairly routine enterprises, and certainly many people are employed, and the economy benefits in great ways as these "execution" focused businesses thrive. We need these types of enterprises if we are to provide for millions in our economy. What Dutch knew, however, is that we also need the risk taker, the "crackpot", the entrepreneurial thinker that will not be satisfied with a copycat business, however lucrative. He may have also known that the sure thing profits may not be so sure, if after the war the volumes decrease, the multi-thousand plane orders disappear, and the skills to be learned by hard knocks in careful experimentation and development were never acquired. A company may find the easy mass manufacturing profits are gone and there are no new product development skills at the ready to be employed in the new paradigm of business. Sometimes the "crackpot" risk taker may not be properly credited for farsightedness.

As the stage is set for a race against time to develop the world's fastest high tech fighter, we are curious about what was in the mind of Dutch as he proposed his own challenge to these procurement officials? Just what "aces" did he hold? Was he privy to knowledge that some others were not? We are aware that he has made trips to British and to German aircraft plants in 1938. What did he file away from these plant trips? What clever ideas has he seen or developed himself that the rest of the industry is not using? What does the team look like that he has assembled for this improbable mission? Has anyone ever succeeded in such a fast track development? How good will he be at negotiating any "wiggle" room if the goal is close, but not quite met at the end of 120 days? How flexible will the British be if the design looks promising but has a few kinks to work out? Will it be faster and can it even withstand the first test flight? The story unfolds.

Just what was the plan Dutch Kindleberger had in mind when he suggested the short fuse design schedule? As it turns out, Dutch knew that North American had completed classified research in cooperation with NACA, the predecessor to NASA, on a new type low drag wing design called the "laminar flow" wing. This had been researched and developed and a paper published. (Selig) He planned to be the first to use this type wing. OK, so there is an academic paper on a test wing profile that shows reduced drag, while still providing adequate lift. But since no one has used this in an actual airplane, it is really unproven technology outside the laboratory. But recall Dutch is an "airplane guy". To him, this is a genuinely original development. It implies that by changing the aerodynamic cross section of the wing, as well as the angle of attack, or wing transverse angle, a lower drag is experienced, thus requiring less power for the same amount of lift force. To an airplane guy, this means he can get any tradeoff combination of more lift or higher speed, for the same expended horsepower! This is a golden opportunity, and it is probable, that although all defense contractors are able to get the report, it is unlikely anyone else is paying attention to this dry research, much less anyone with the power to make any significant business decisions. This knowledge must be one of his "aces".

The second "ace" was his design team. He had J.L. Lee Atwood, his old friend as the chief engineer, but he also had two key aircraft designers, Raymond Rice and Edgar Schmued. (Kinzey, 1996, p.5) Schmued had been with German manufacturers Fokker and Messerschmitt in 1925. He knew his team would see this design challenge as a great adventure. They immediately began the detailed design process and worked day and night as a team for 102 days to develop the design into a finished prototype without an engine. Every expedient imaginable was taken to accelerate the project. It is on record that the wheels were borrowed from an AT-6 Trainer. Exactly 47 days after the airframe is completed, the plane flew with the Allison V-1710-39 engine. It did indeed exceed the speed of the P-40. (Kinzey, 1996, p.5) And lo and behold, it had the greatest range, or greatest fuel efficiency, of any fighter at the time. The maximum range was now over 1,650 miles with added external wing tanks as compared to the P-40 with 650 miles. (Green and Swanborough, 2001) (Loftin, 2006) The laminar flow wing technology was proven! It resulted in a huge increase in fuel efficiency, due to the greatly reduced drag coefficient of the wing profile. The lower force of drag also resulted in higher maximum speed, 20 mph faster in the first version. The maneuverability and stability were excellent. The low altitude performance with the Allison single stage supercharged engine was fine. In fact, the only significant drawback was the poor high altitude performance, because the engine specified for this first prototype was the low altitude version of the Allison engine. This was the version with a single stage supercharger. This of course limited the high altitude power. However, the plane is delivered with the low altitude Allison engines and proves perfectly satisfactory, and quite superior in speed, efficiency and range to the P-40. The plane is put into service for close air support and other low altitude applications. The British are delighted with their gamble paying off.

The Battle of Britain (July –October, 1940) was won without much help from the Mustang, as it was only a lower altitude fighter in 1940. The US is brought into the war the day after the Pearl Harbor Attack, which occurred on December 7th, 1941. By the time the U.S. is geared up into the war, in 1942, bombing runs on Europe and eventually Germany are begun. The later bombing flights into Germany are so long that there is no fighter with the range to escort the bombers for the full length of the missions. The fighters escort for most of the distance, then have to turn back before they get near Germany. The bombing runs over Germany are a key strategy to defeating the Axis powers. It is an attempt to destroy the German war supply machine. Great numbers of planes and pilots are being lost because there are no long range fighter escorts. It is the intention that near air superiority be achieved before the ground invasion and liberation of France is launched. Meanwhile, ground campaigns are won in North Africa, and Sicily. The Italian campaign is under way before the D-Day invasion of France.

Some understanding of the technology of piston engine aircraft of the day is required to fully appreciate the development path for this fighter. As altitude gets above 15,000 ft, in order to maintain power output, the thinner air requires some type of pre-charge compressor to increase the air density prior to admission into the engine. Either a supercharger or a turbocharger is required to pre-compress the air. A supercharger is a compressor that is mechanically driven, through a gear by the engine. A turbocharger uses the high temperature, high energy, waste exhaust air flow to power a turbine expansion wheel which then drives the compressor wheel. Because of the extreme thinness of the air at high altitude, two stages of compression are required to support adequate pre-charge compression. A single stage unit is simply inadequate, whether a supercharger or a turbocharger.

The Allison engine designers chose to use a single stage supercharger in their standard engine for lower altitude service. The Allison engine option for extreme high altitude use was a "turbosupercharger", or turbocharger. The added turbocharger provided the extra second stage of compression necessary for extreme high altitude service. The only drawback was that the turbine side of the turbocharger requires a special chrome steel to withstand the high exhaust temperature. The chromium required was a scarce metal in wartime, so the only aircraft getting the Allison engines with high altitude turbochargers were the high altitude bombers. Practically none were allocated to fighters.

There is one engine that is known to be widely available to the allies for high altitude flight, and that is the Rolls Royce, linear, V-12, water cooled, supercharged Merlin V-1650. This engine uses a two stage supercharger. Since the two stage supercharger does not require the scarce chromium content steel, it is a readily available engine option. The conventional steels used in the Rolls Royce super charger are common and there is no limit to their production.

Almost as soon as the original orders are delivered, the obvious next improvement of securing a means to provide for high altitude performance enhancement began. The obvious choice was to install the two-stage supercharged Rolls Royce Merlin engine. In the U.S., Packard is licensed to manufacture the Merlin engine, and an effort is underway to install this engine in prototypes. The British have begun to do the same with the Rolls Royce manufactured Merlin. It is debated who thought of the idea first. Because the airframe is so efficient, everyone understands that once the Merlin engine is installed, this fighter will be the longest range high altitude fighter in the world.

It is late '43 when the high altitude version is prototyped and flown. Later, some modifications to the cockpit bubble are introduced to provide greater visibility. By the time the high altitude enhanced Mustangs are introduced into the European theatre, it is the winter of '43-'44, and the need for a long range, high altitude bomber escort is acute. With the introduction of the Merlin engine equipped Mustang, bombers can now be escorted all the way from bases in England to German targets and back. The top speed of the Mustang is also increased with the new engine, and a 4 bladed propeller is introduced. The Mustang is so effective as a long range bomber escort, that within a few months, near air superiority is achieved. (Ethell and Sand, 2002, p.126) (Caldwell and Muller, 2007, P.162-163) The plane is outmatching the best of the Luftwaffe and the combination of damage to parts factories and airfields is taking a huge toll on the enemy's ability to defend its skies.

The D-Day invasion can go on in June of '44 rather than waiting another entire year. This is actually an incredible achievement. The successful conquest of the air enables the ground invasion to proceed and saves many lives on D-Day. Brutal though it was, it would have been much worse, and possibly even turned back, had there been any significant Luftwaffe air attacks. (Ethell and Sand, 2002, p.126) The dominance of the air gives the Allies such a powerful advantage that the ground war is enabled to proceed much faster. Even the German superiority in tanks is also partly counterbalanced by this dominance of the air, as there are several planes that are useful tank killers.

The role the Mustang played in securing this air dominance is unquestioned. In the European theatre alone, it scored 4,950 aircraft downed in aerial combat and 4,131 destroyed on the ground. (Glancey, 2006, p.188) That was more than any other fighter in the European theater. It destroyed so many German fighters that pilots became a scarce resource.

By the war's end, over 16,700 Mustangs had been built. The final version, P-51D, was a sleek and nimble aircraft that looked as fast as it flew. The 360 degree visibility provided by the bubble canopy was a welcome improvement. This was Chuck Yeager's and many other pilots' ace producing aircraft. The Mustang was even used successfully in ground support in Korea and the Vietnam conflict. Air forces of more than 55 nations were supported with this aircraft. (Gunston, 1984, p. 58) Pilots loved it so much that it helped inspire the post WWII commemorative air force effort across the US.

What are the leadership lessons to be learned from this risky, yet successful venture in aircraft design? Are there life lessons as well wrapped up in this story? Certainly we can take away a respect for the judgment of Dutch Kindleberger, an awe of the design team skill and work ethic, and admiration for the innovation of the designers in converting to the high altitude engine, which arguably accelerated the ending of the war. But what is a modern day executive, manager, or design decision maker to learn from this as a case study? Let us examine the risk management issue next.

Chuck Yeager's "Glamorous Glen III", a P51D, 8th AF/357thFG/363rd FS, aircraft in which he scored several of his 12.5 kills, including two Me262 jets

North American NA-73X, first model prototype

XP-51 Early model for testing provided to USAAC

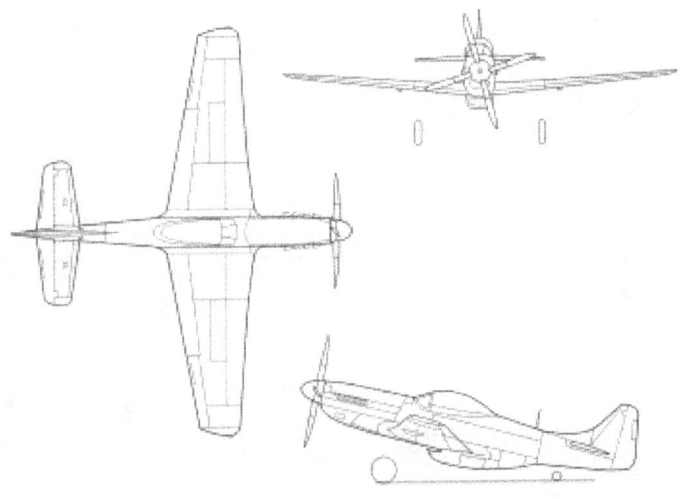

Line Drawing of P-51

Pilots of the all African American 332nd Fighter Group at Ramitelli, Italy, from left: Lt. Dempsey W. Morgan, Lt. Carol S. Woods, Lt. Robert H. Nelron, Jr., Capt. Andrew D. Turner, and Lt. Clarence P. Lester

P-51 Takes off from Iwo Jima

P-51's being loaded onto aircraft carrier for transport to Korea

P-51D, 374th Fighter Squadron, early D model

P-51 Mustangs in Republic of Korea (South) Air Force

P-51 Assembly Inglewood, California

Republic of China P-51s

Chapter 3

The Analysis of the Decision

Risk management is one of the desirable skills sought after when hiring decision makers. But how is it evaluated? How is it determined that someone is good at making crucial decisions under uncertainty? That is how real world business, industry, and even warfare really works…..decisions must be made under uncertainty. There is no point in waiting for perfect data. Data is always limited, and sometimes in error. How did Dutch really know what to do? Was it completely intuitive, or is there a calculus that can determine the correct course of action a large portion of the time? There are many computer programs offered today that will assist in determining some probabilities of certain random events, and these bear some study and review. However, we know these were not part of the tool kit Dutch used to make his decision. Perhaps there is a protocol we can derive that will assist the modern manager wade through the reams of data, "Monte Carlo" simulation program outputs, and plethora of consultants ready to offer advice. Let us examine the decision and its implications in this chapter.

The offer presented to Dutch Kindleberger, as President of North American Aviation, in 1940, was an enviable one. British procurement officials were simply asking them to subcontract the manufacture of the P-40, for which they would receive a fee to cover all costs as well as provide a handsome profit. It was basically a no lose proposition, guaranteed profits for simply doing what they knew how to do, build airplanes. For most managers, this is an obvious decision, right? It is still the throes of a depression nationwide, and these profits are necessary to keep the company solvent and viable. The payments are even guaranteed, if not directly, at least indirectly through the US Lend Lease Act which is a way for a neutral country, as the USA, to support England and other countries in the fight against the Axis powers. So this is as close to a risk free return as can ever be expected by a CEO. On the one hand we have a nearly 100% certainty of profit for this course of action, and any alternate course will involve less certainty, with varying degrees of reward, depending on the outcome scenario assumed.

Attractive though this offer is, Dutch wishes to have his firm design a new airframe , and use this to not only fulfill the contract order requirement, but also to exceed the expectations for performance, and thus be able to acquire further orders as a new fighter with improved capabilities. However, there is risk associated with this endeavor, so a probability of success as well as an estimate of expected return of each possible outcome must be determined in order to evaluate alternatives.

Using the conventional expected value analysis technique, we can review the options viewed from the perspective of a CEO faced with alternative choices. That is, we multiply the assumed probability by the value associated with that outcome to get an "expected value". All alternative assigned probabilities must sum to unity. This technique, though simple, is the fundamental basis for risk analysis. It also is simple enough to use to bridge between the intuitive, or "gut feel" method of decision analysis and the more objective mathematical models. We will attempt to understand this decision analysis method with two goals in mind, that the protocol used must be mathematically sound, and that the assumptions used must be intuitively acceptable. When decisions can mean the success or failure of a company, many jobs created or lost, or perhaps greater consequences, the entire methodology must be credible and even unassailable. It must, in other words, "pass the laugh test". We need to learn to use this mathematical tableau method in such a way as to be intuitively acceptable and easy to apply.

As an example of the simple expected value analysis, consider the two choice alternative outline of as to whether to simply build the P-40 fighters as requested, for the guaranteed profit, or try to develop a fighter that is superior and acceptable to the British in a limited time frame. If we assume that there is only a 35 percent chance that the development will be successful, and we have data regarding the profit for each successful option, we can construct a hypothetical decision analysis using expected value techniques to obtain an analytical answer. Assume a guaranteed profit per plane of $7,000 for subcontract fabrication, and a slightly higher ultimate profit margin, $10,000, for a homegrown design.

Profit per plane X Probability of Success = Expected Value

Option A : Build the P-40 $7,000 X 1.0 = $7,000

Option B : Build P-51

   1) Successful Design $10,000 X .35 = $3,500

   2) Unsuccessful Design $-0- X .65 = $--0--

     Sum probabilities Option B P= 1.0

        Option B Expected Value   = $3,500

This is the conventional basic expected value tableau. Notice the entire analysis hinges on the assumption of the expected probability, P, of success for the new design. This of course is a subjective judgment, and no matter what technique we use to assess the probability of success, our analysis at some point must make some kind of judgment about this success probability. These assumptions can be hidden in a complex array of alternate probabilities, and options within options, even computer generated random numbers regarding various random event options within given scenarios, but ultimately there must be an assignment of probability, and an agreement on how it is derived. Thus even with Monte Carlo simulations, somewhere, somehow, there is an agreement on the mechanism of assignment of this value, which in itself is a judgment. By this over simplified analysis, we get the obvious answer that the expected values indicate that the sure bet contract should be taken.

We get the same answer, until the assumed probability of success rises to 70%, at such time the alternatives are mathematically equal. This technique is so intuitively acceptable, that we assume that at some subconscious level, it was used by Dutch to assist in his decision. As the numbers are approximately reasonably correct for this scenario, based on historical knowledge of the contract costs for planes during this era, we see that this analysis is probably still missing something. What? Did he just have a greater than 70% assessment of new design success probability? Even if his assessment of success was 80%, we are only $1,000 per plane, or 16% more profitable than the no risk option, still a somewhat shaky decision. Something is missing...............executives are called upon to make decisions like this all the time, with similar subtleties in the data, assumptions that are only hopeful guesses, and vaguely defined options that are often also not quite fixed in detail. How does a successful decision maker think, and what makes the difference between their analysis techniques and the methodical engineer or risk analyst with their array of analytical programs and tools?

We are also reminded of this great truth, no one gets it right all the time. The greatest practitioners do still make mistakes, and try to learn from them. But don't we wish to have a high percentage of good decisions? Aren't we after a key element in the decision making process that will consistently support our decisions so that they will be right the vast majority of the time? Or are we doomed to be like the golfer who occasionally hits a terrific shot or has a great game day, but later doesn't know why and can't repeat it at will?

Perhaps there are clues to this mystery in the results of the decision.

The business aspects of the decision are a great place to start the review. Recall that the request to subcontract the P-40's probably involved a quantity of planes in the area of 2,000 unit count. If the profit per plane was in the $7,000 range, the potential value to the company in pretax profit may have been in the $14,000,000 range. The alternate expected profit per plane from an internal design may have been in the range of $10,000 per plane. The expectation might also be that if the design were sufficiently better than the P-40, there might be additional new orders, prompted by the desire to simply buy the best available technology. How many sales could be projected based on that successful design scenario? Maybe 6,000, or 8,000, or possibly even 10,000 units? 8,000 units would result in a pretax profit of approximately $80MM. This would be huge compared to the $14 MM expected from the first subcontract offer. So something of a potential might exist to look at an alternate upside to the successful design that we didn't include in our first simplistic setup. So perhaps we should revise the options to reflect three scenarios in the tableau that represent the possible outcomes from the internal design option. An alternate third case could be considered with this high potential profit, but also a probability of success revised to reflect the 3-way split in probable outcomes, say a 30 percent probability of failure, a 60 percent probability of modest success and a 10 per cent probability of great success, to look something like this:

Option A: Build P-40's 2,000 X $7,0000 X 1.0 = **$14MM**

Option B: Build P-51's

   1) Failed design   2,000 X   0   X 0.3 =   0

   2) Modest success 2,000 X $10,000 x 0.6 = $12MM

   3) Great success   8,000 X $10,000 X 0.1 = $8MM

   　　Total Expected Value Option B   = **$20MM**

Now the scenario begins to favor the more risky venture of designing a new plane. Note that even with only a 10% chance of great success, the expected value is higher than the no risk path. Also note that even if only modest success is attained, the actual expected profits for modest success exceed the conventional subcontract profit, $20 MM, ($10,000 per plane at 2,000 planes) versus $14 MM. So perhaps part of the inadequacy of our first decision framework was our failure to visualize the extent of the upside, if we have great success.

Note, however, this particular lesson is even more powerful when we examine the actual results of this design. There were actually much more than 8,000 units built by the end of the war, rather over 16,000 units were built! So the actual approximate pretax profit for the North American Aviation Company would be approximately $160,000,000 in 1945 dollars!

So let us lay out a decision tableau in hindsight to see what may have been a better layout of the potential for this decision.

Option A: Build P-40's 2,000 X $7,000 X 1.0 = ***$14MM***

Option B: Build P-51's

   1) Failed design   2,000 X   0   X 0.3 =   0

   2) Modest success   2,000 X $10,000 X 0.6 = $12MM

   3) Great success   8,000 X $10,000 X 0.05= $4MM

   4) Raging success   16,000 X $10,000 X 0.05= $8MM

      Total Expected Value Option B   = ***$24MM***

Even using the modest probability of only 5% of "Raging" success (20:1 odds against) , and only 5% probability of "great" success, and including a 30% probability of failure, the resultant expected value in a hindsight back-testing analysis is $24MM! If the "raging " success is actually achieved, a potential pretax profit might be in the $160 MM range, compared to the actual best guaranteed pretax profit for subcontract manufacture of $14 MM!

We can clearly see from this hindsight analysis that one of the keys used by successful leaders in decisions under uncertainty may be that the vision of potential success is opened up to include perhaps a more realistic view of the upside. However, had Dutch communicated this potential and even so much as mentioned the upside even close to this kind of number prior to his decision, many may have thought him unfit to lead for having such "delusional" thoughts.

Here enters the key word not to be ignored when reviewing the concept of decisions under uncertainty, ***leader***. There is a great difference between a leader and a manager. Both are needed in our world, and the basic decisions of everyday actions are well served by simple, straightforward views as illustrated in the first tableau. We just need to execute our plans well and follow the routine choices, and that is really all that is required to have good track record of wise choices in life and success. However, at some level, and in certain times, there is a need for real leadership which requires a vision of the future that is so optimistic it is borderline delusional!

Is it wise to discuss "delusional" leadership as if it is virtuous? Or is it a fairly common weakness in management, as with many of us as individuals, that we find it difficult to visualize raging success, and if we can, we dare not speak it for fear of ostracizing ourselves and being relegated to the role of "dreamer", unstable and not quite fit for middle management, much less upper management critical leadership roles?

Has our training and education helped us find good tools for routine decisions that could easily be delegated to lower levels? Are our days are spent troubling over these important, yet straightforward decisions, because it is so much easier than facing the difficult task of taking on greater challenge with its attendant risk? Is there power in this type of thought process where extreme success is contemplated as a remote, but possible outcome? .

Chapter 4

Bold and Virtuous Leadership Lessons

The concept of visualizing extreme success as a potential outcome, boldness in examining our alternatives and the brutally difficult task of admitting to ourselves our great fear of failure is powerful. When examined together, a powerful insight is revealed. Could this offer clues as to the genius behind visionary leaders such as Dutch Kindleberger and others who were able to truly achieve great things in their service to their organizations, their country, and even mankind?

The results of analyses such as this are often considered "radioactive", "delusional", or otherwise simply dangerous.

As we try to gain some benefit for our organizations as well as our own careers, we will struggle to know just how and when to apply the protocol of upsizing the upside. But perhaps the most important judgment call is not assessing the potential of the upside, but rather correctly assessing the magnitude and probability of the downside, worst case. This is because it is the downside and a realistic probability of its occurrence that really serves to limit the risk we assume in attempting to reach the upside, outsized, best case. It is often the overestimate of the downside consequence and or probability of occurring that drives our decisions to be more conservative.

Summarizing the lessons of this analysis............

1) **Understand the issue**- Try to understand as much as you can about the business element or issue under review. Make an effort to fully understand the technology, if at all possible. At least try get a clear executive summary of the technology if it is a technical area under discussion. Do the walking around necessary to see beyond the formal briefings or reports. Try to understand the field level details of the issue, human factors, technological weaknesses, etc.
2) **Have some passion about the issue**- Find something positive in the business or effort being undertaken by seeing the good it does for society, or the negative things it removes. Imagine the potential benefits of success in more than one dimension, more than the money involved, the supply of some need at a lower cost, an uplifting of some quality of life element, etc.
3) **Get expert help**- When Dutch pushed forward with his decision, he was in the

possession of advanced design knowledge from the wing research. He also knew he had the best design team in the industry. Recklessness is not being advocated here. He was a professional in the prime of his life, supported by the same. He simply chose the more difficult, challenging path.

4) **Evaluate realistically the downside potential and probability**- We must understand the potential of the worst case scenario, especially if risk to human safety or health is in play. We would not want to encourage reckless risks. Extreme conservatism is a virtue in protecting health, safety, and the environment. If, however the business involved does not have appreciable risks in this regard, or the issues in question are separate from the health and safety elements of the business, then an honest evaluation of the potential economic losses or lost opportunities should be assessed. The goal of this evaluation is to understand the magnitude of the impact of a complete failure of the effort undertaken. Be brutally honest. Look realistically at the probability of this downside occurring.

5) **Evaluate realistically the potential of a raging success**- Open up your imagination to the extreme potential of the upside, be borderline "delusional". Then assign a realistically low probability to this potential outcome. What is the very best that could happen, and how likely is it?

The idea of a business decision maker having great impact on the good of society by being at once bold and virtuous is a powerful one. When coupled with the tools to make decisions under uncertainty well, the potential good can be amazing.

Works Cited

Caldwell, Donald, and Richard Muller. *The Luftwaffe Over Germany - Defense of the Third Reich*. St.Paul, Minnesota: Greenhill Books, MBI Publishing, 2007. ISBN 978-185367-712-0

Ethell, Jeffrey, and Robert Sand. *World War II Fighter*. Minneapolis, Minnesota: Zenith Imprint, 2002. ISBN 978-0-7603-135-4

Glancey, Johnathan. *Spitfire: The Illustrated Biography*. London: Atlantic Books, 2006. ISBN 978-1-84354-528-6

Green, William and Gordon Swanborough. *The Great Book Of Fighters*. St. Paul, Minnesota: MBI Publishing, 2001. ISBN 0-7603-1194-3

Gunston, Bill. *Aerei della* seconda *Guerra modiale (in Italian)*. Milan:Peruzzo editore, 1984. No ISBN

Kinzey, Bert. *P-51 Mustang in Detail & Scale: Part 1; Prototype Through P-51C.* Carrolton, Texas:

Detail and Scale Inc., 1996. ISBN 1-888974-02-8

Loftin, L.K., Jr. *Quest for Performance: The Evolution of Modern Aircraft, NASA SP-468*, Washington, D.C.: NASA History Office, Retrieved: 22 April 2006

Pearcy, Arthur. *Lend – Lease Aircraft of World War II*. Shrewsbury, UK: Airlife Publishing Ltd., 1996. ISBN 1-85310-443-4

Selig, Michael. "P51-D Wingroot Section." UIUC.edu. Retrieved: 22 March 2008, Web source

www.ingramcontent.com/pod-product-compliance
Lightning Source LLC
Chambersburg PA
CBHW071824170526
45167CB00003B/1415